Christmas Favorites

for Two

ISBN-13: 978-1-4234-1366-0
ISBN-10: 1-4234-1366-0

HAL•LEONARD®
CORPORATION
7777 W. BLUEMOUND RD. P.O. BOX 13819 MILWAUKEE, WI 53213

Visit Hal Leonard Online at
www.halleonard.com

CAROLING, CAROLING

SECONDO

Words by WIHLA HUTSON
Music by ALFRED BURT

With a lilt

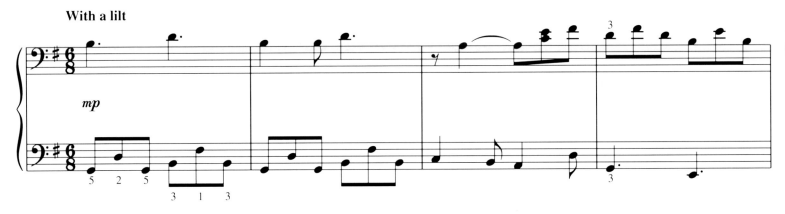

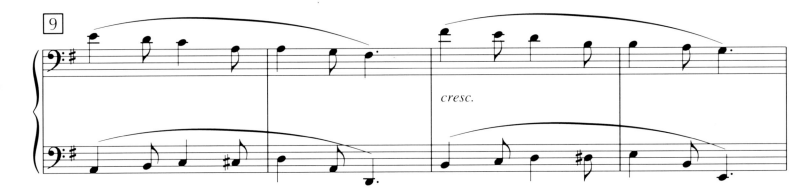

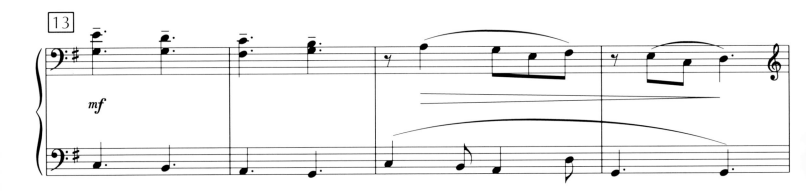

CAROLING, CAROLING

PRIMO

Words by WIHLA HUTSON
Music by ALFRED BURT

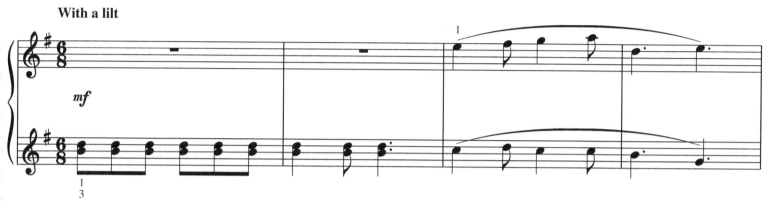

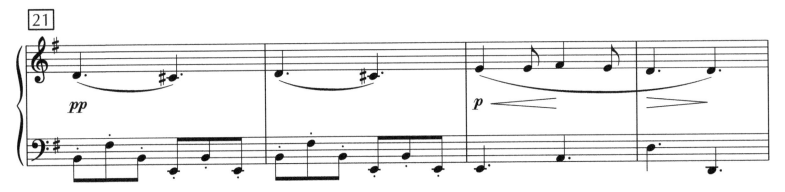

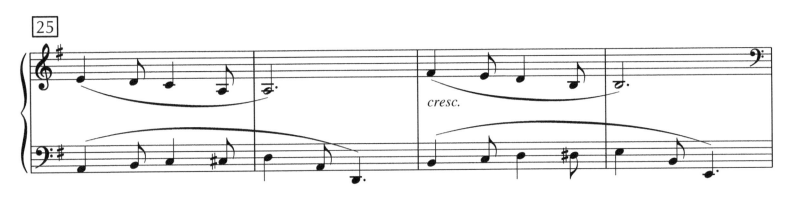

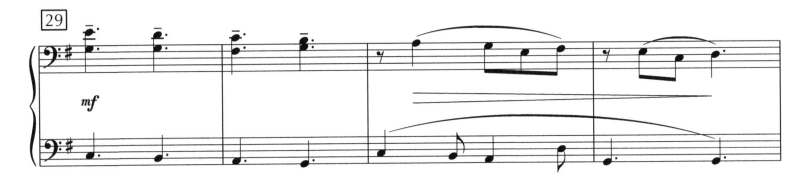

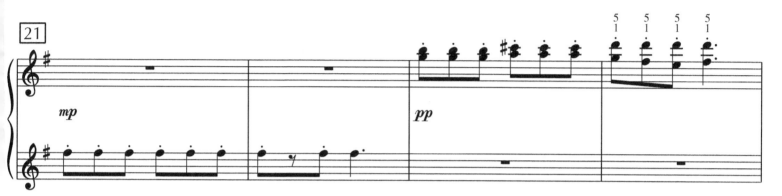

CHRISTMAS TIME IS HERE

from A CHARLIE BROWN CHRISTMAS

SECONDO

Words by LEE MENDELSON
Music by VINCE GUARALDI

CHRISTMAS TIME IS HERE

from A CHARLIE BROWN CHRISTMAS

PRIMO

Words by LEE MENDELSON
Music by VINCE GUARALDI

SECONDO

DO YOU HEAR WHAT I HEAR

SECONDO

Words and Music by NOEL REGNEY
and GLORIA SHAYNE

Moderately

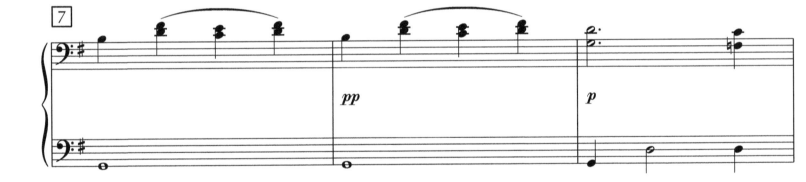

DO YOU HEAR WHAT I HEAR

PRIMO

Words and Music by NOEL REGNEY
and GLORIA SHAYNE

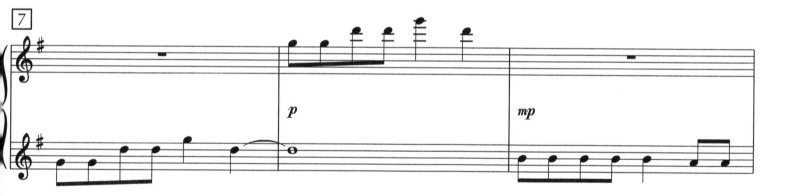

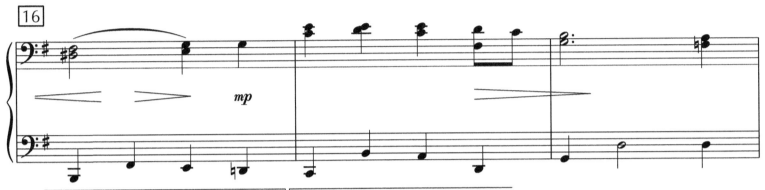

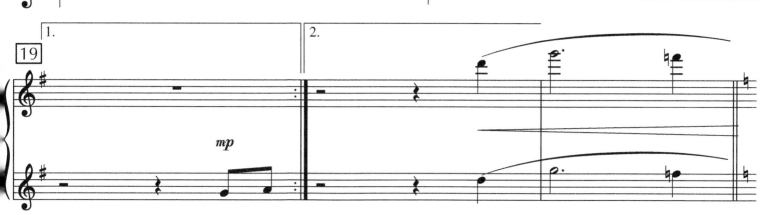

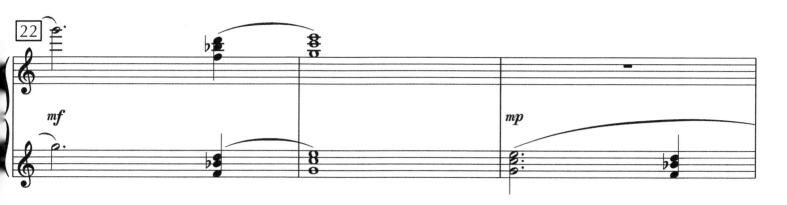

SECONDO

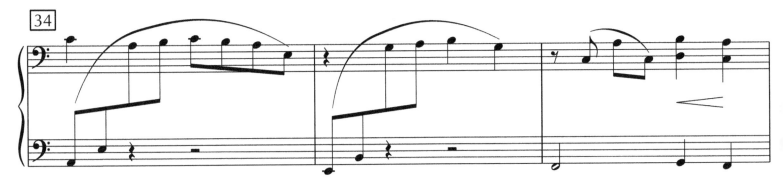

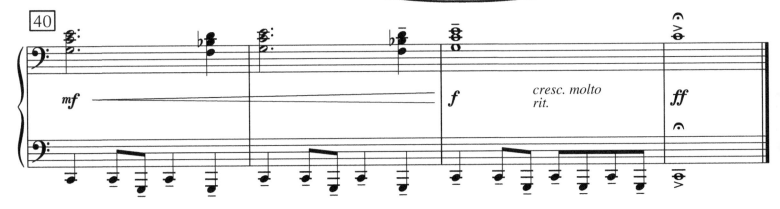

PRIMO

HERE COMES SANTA CLAUS
(Right Down Santa Claus Lane)

SECONDO

Words and Music by GENE AUTRY
and OAKLEY HALDEMAN

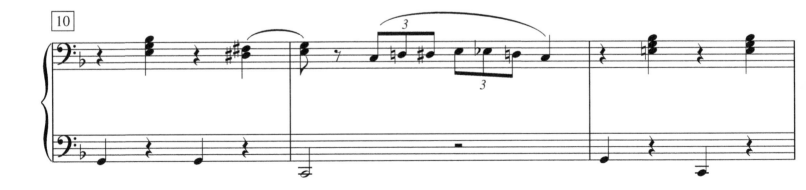

HERE COMES SANTA CLAUS
(Right Down Santa Claus Lane)

PRIMO

Words and Music by GENE AUTRY
and OAKLEY HALDEMAN

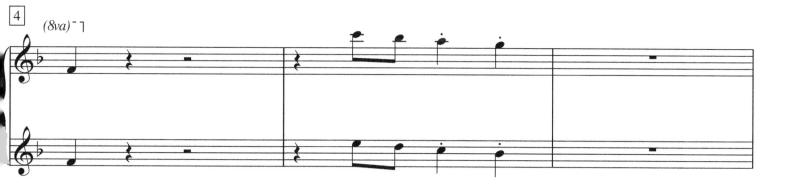

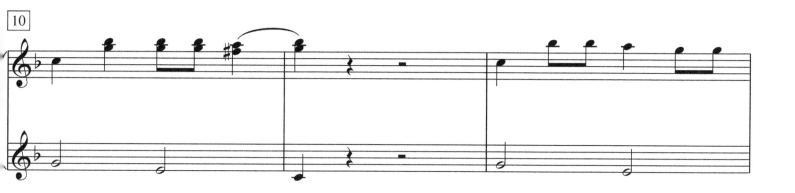

SECONDO

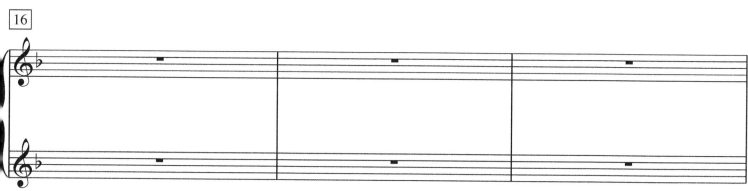

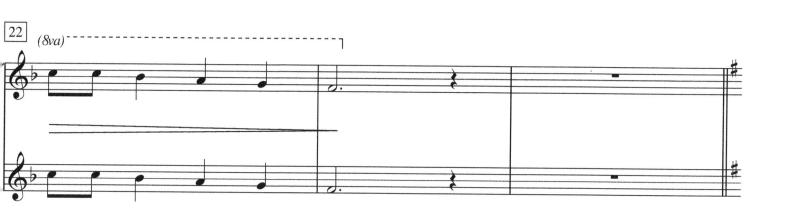

SECONDO

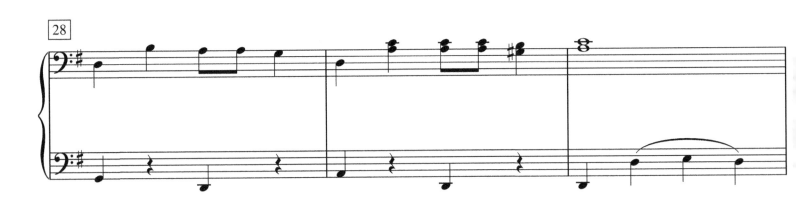

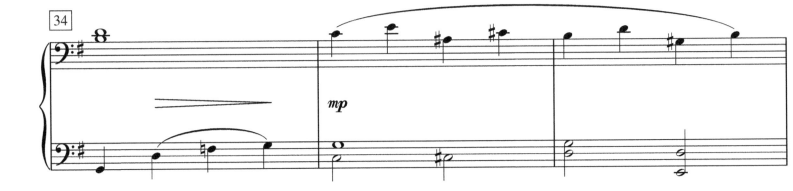

PRIMO

SECONDO

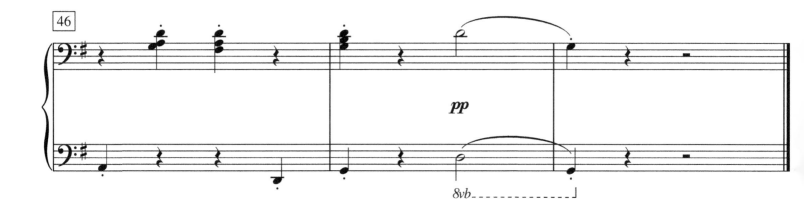

PRIMO

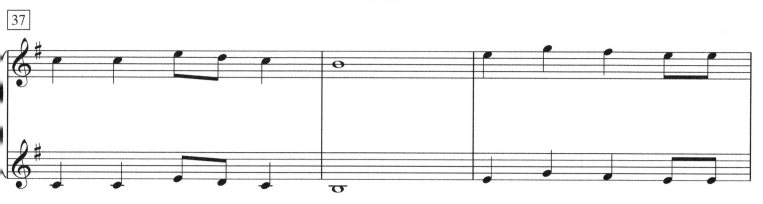

(There's No Place Like)
HOME FOR THE HOLIDAYS

SECONDO

Words by AL STILLMAN
Music by ROBERT ALLEN

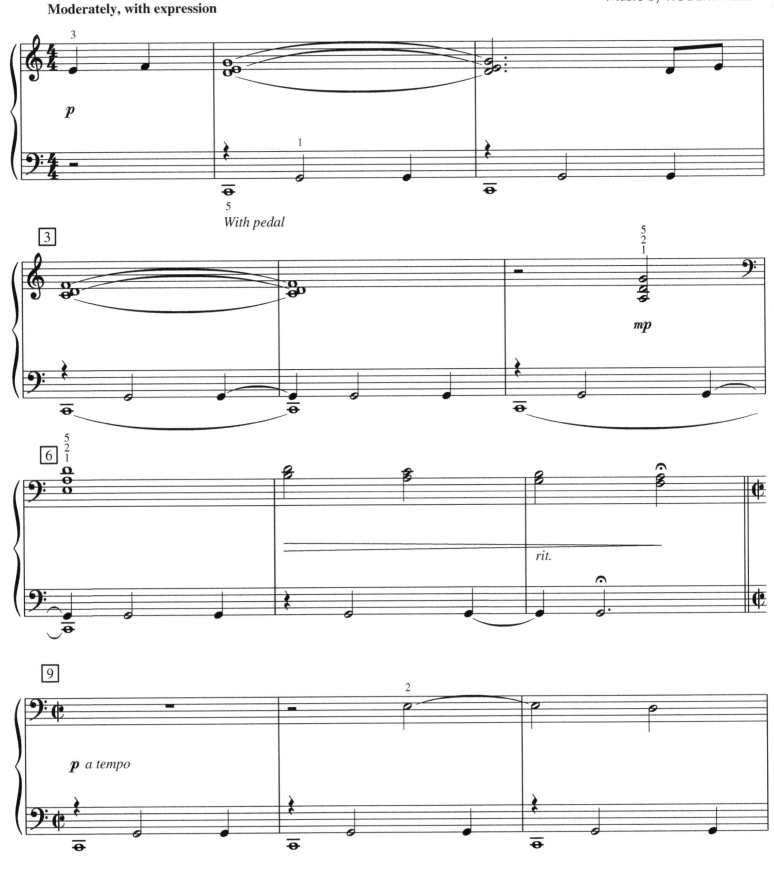

(There's No Place Like)
HOME FOR THE HOLIDAYS

PRIMO

Words by AL STILLMAN
Music by ROBERT ALLEN

Moderately, with expression

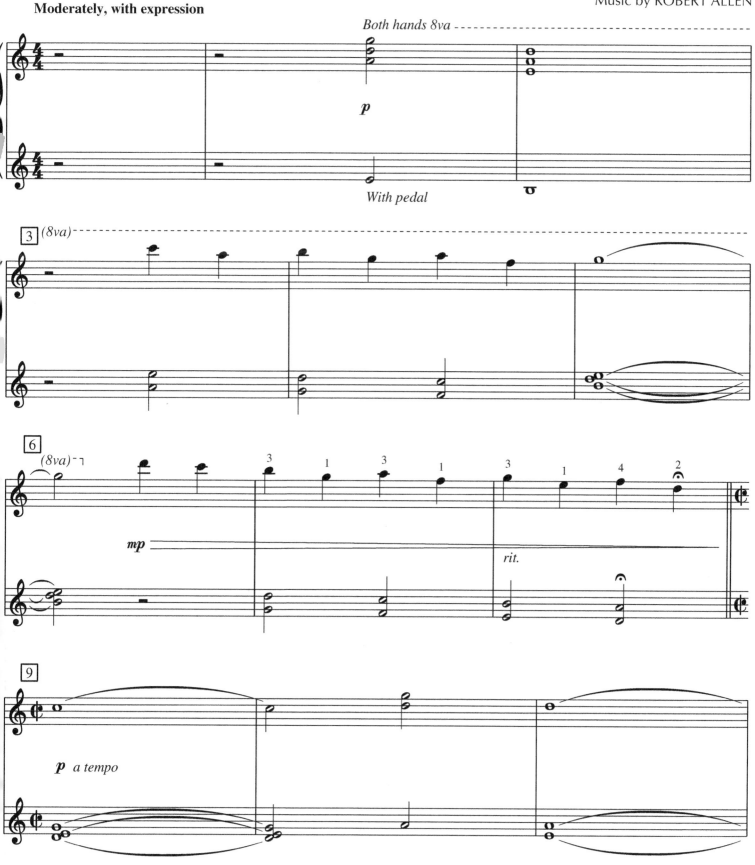

SECONDO

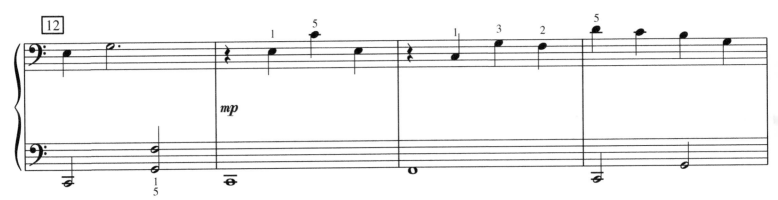

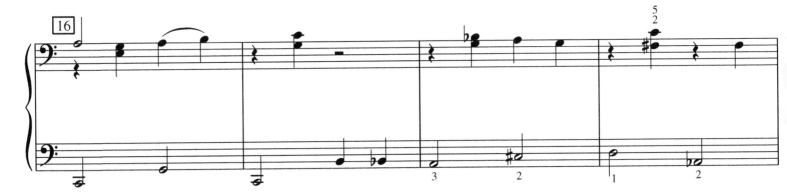

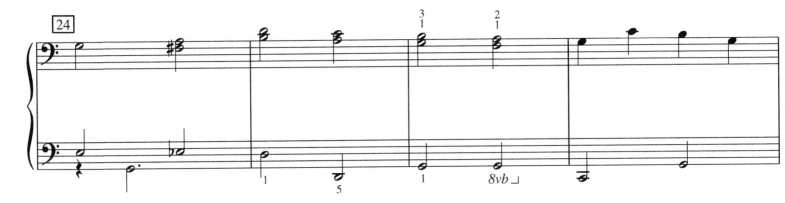

PRIMO

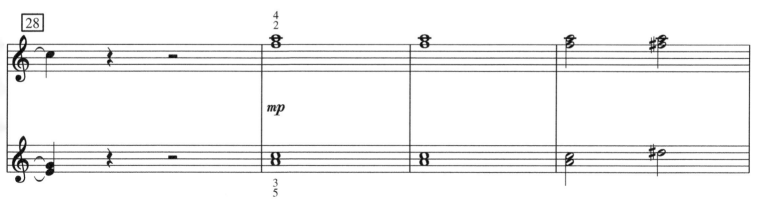

SECONDO

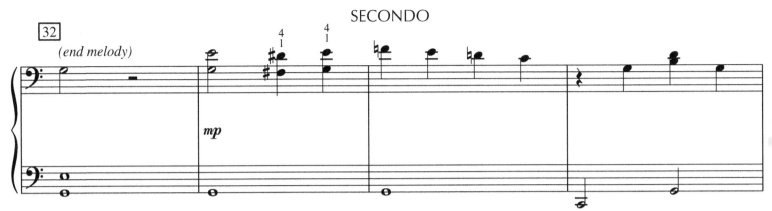

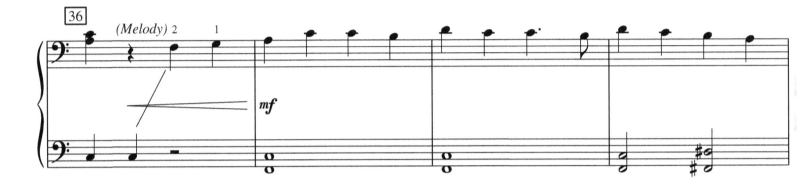

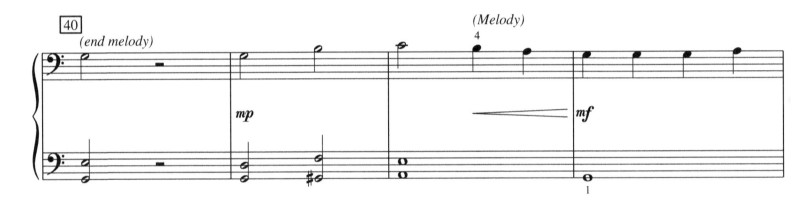

PRIMO

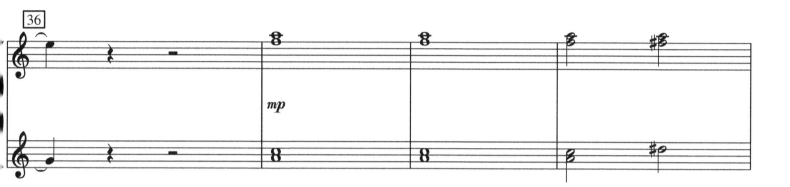

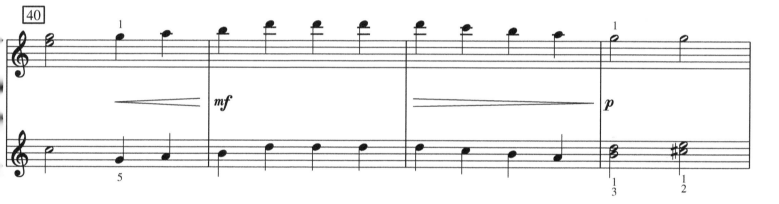

SECONDO

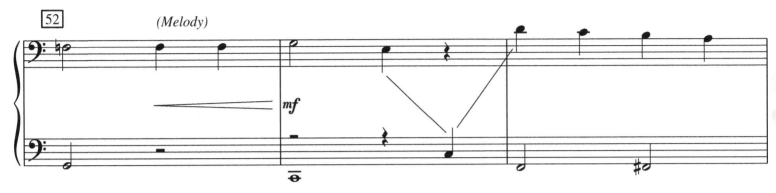

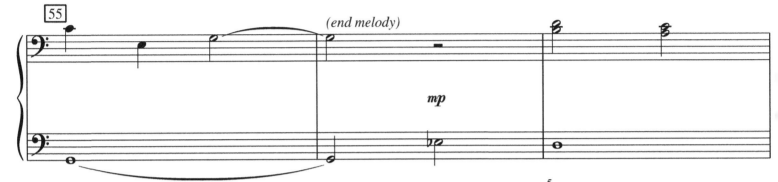

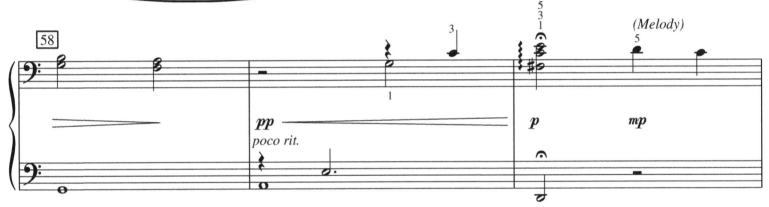

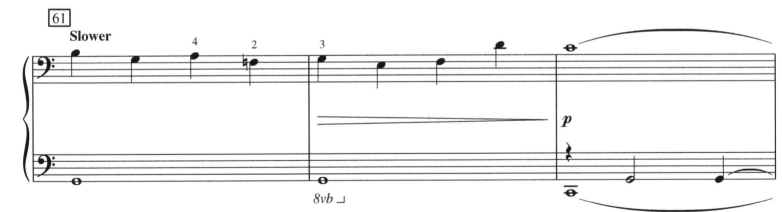

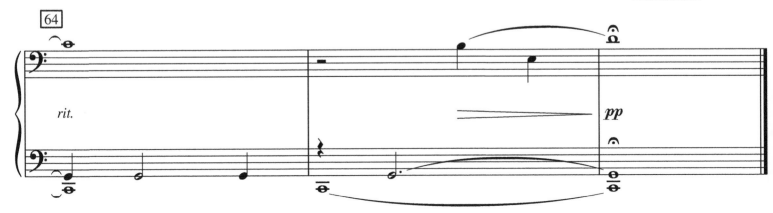

PRIMO

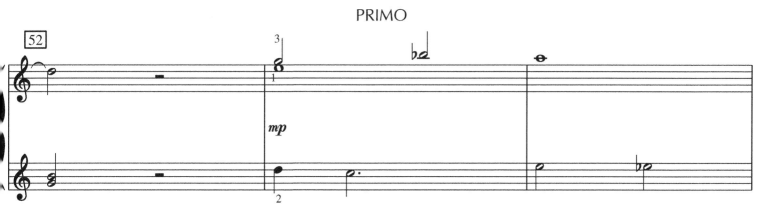

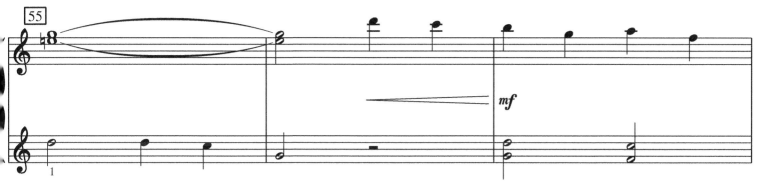

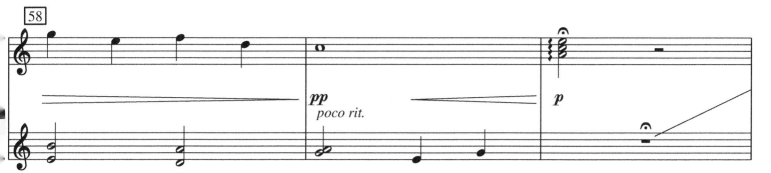

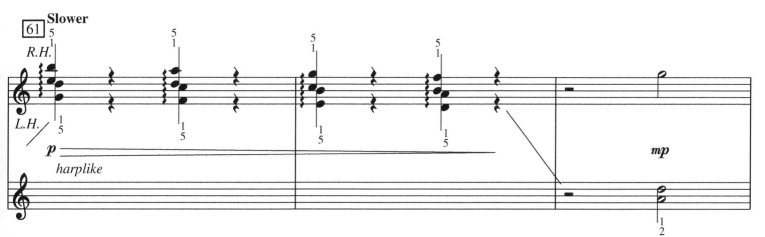

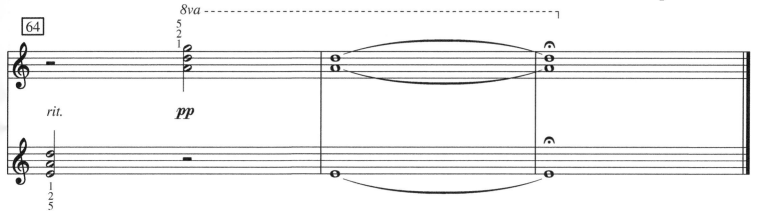

LITTLE SAINT NICK

SECONDO

Words and Music by BRIAN WILSON
and MIKE LOVE

LITTLE SAINT NICK

PRIMO

Words and Music by BRIAN WILSON
and MIKE LOVE

SECONDO

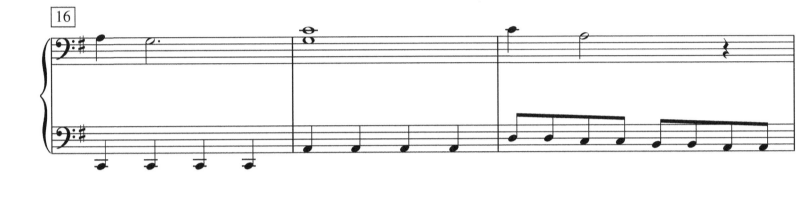

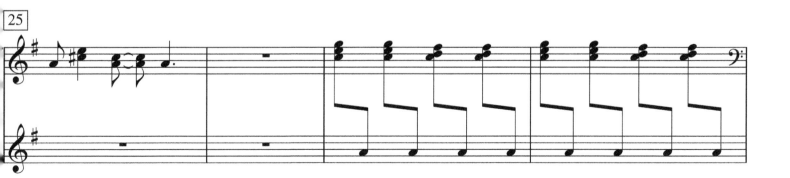

SECONDO

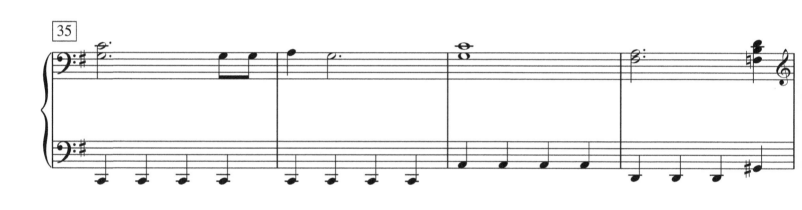

PRIMO

R.H. 8va to end

MERRY CHRISTMAS, DARLING

SECONDO

Words and Music by RICHARD CARPENTER
and FRANK POOLER

With expression

With pedal

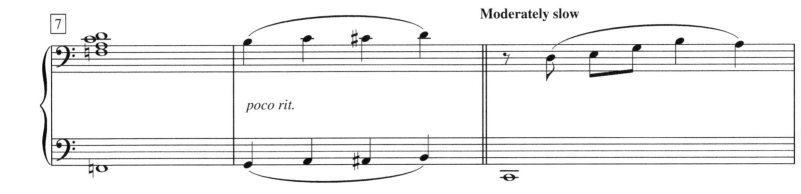

poco rit.

Moderately slow

MERRY CHRISTMAS, DARLING

PRIMO

Words and Music by RICHARD CARPENTER
and FRANK POOLER

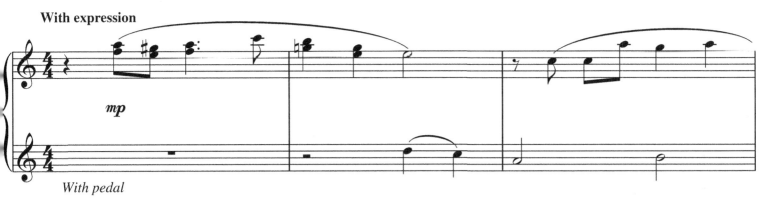

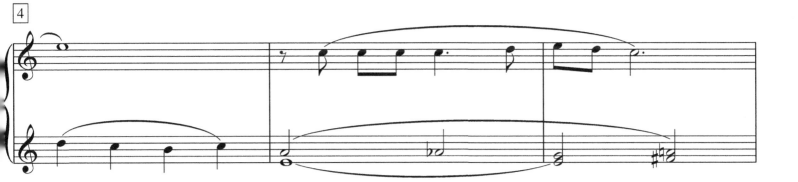

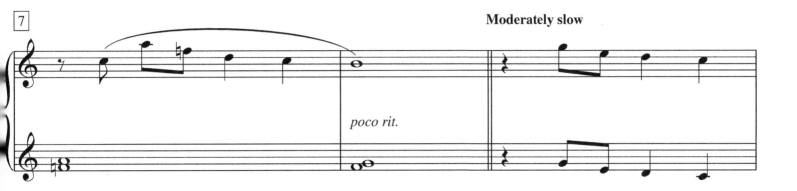

SECONDO

PRIMO

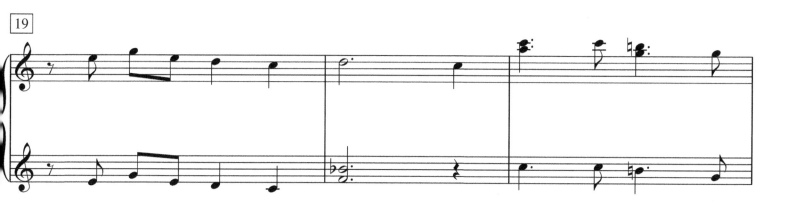

PRIMO

SECONDO

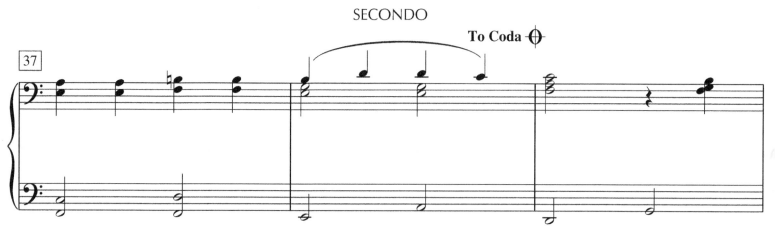

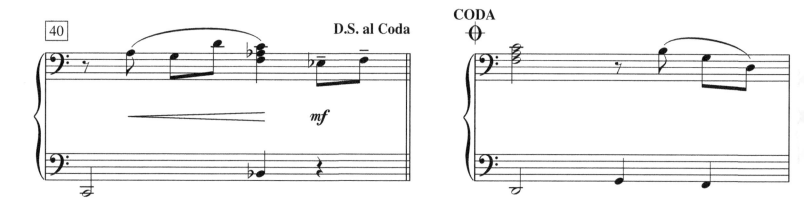

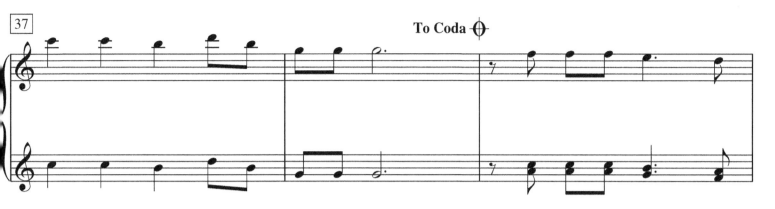

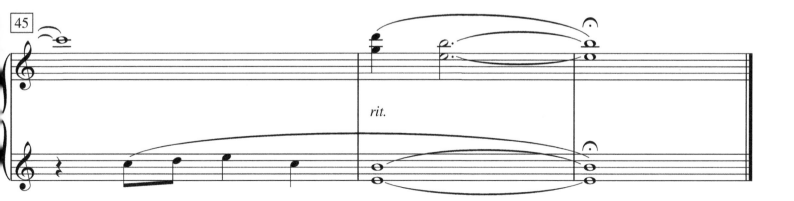

SANTA CLAUS IS COMIN' TO TOWN

SECONDO

Words by HAVEN GILLESPIE
Music by J. FRED COOTS

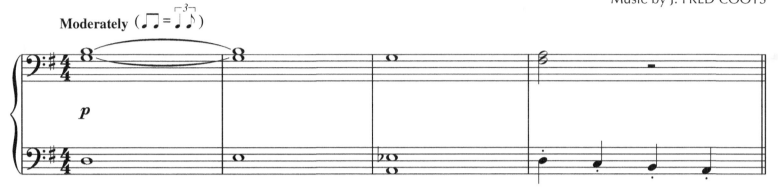

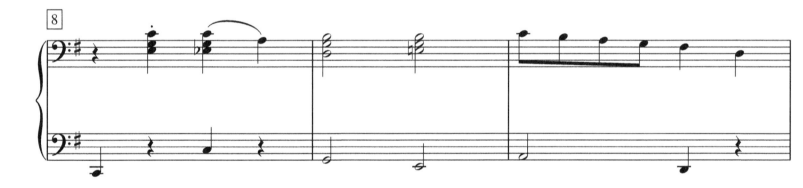

SANTA CLAUS IS COMIN' TO TOWN

PRIMO

Words by HAVEN GILLESPIE
Music by J. FRED COOTS

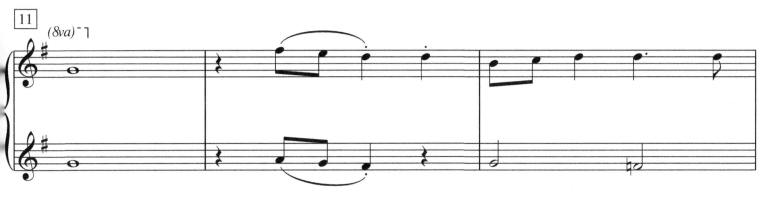

SECONDO

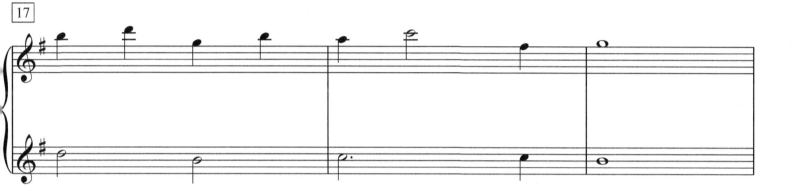

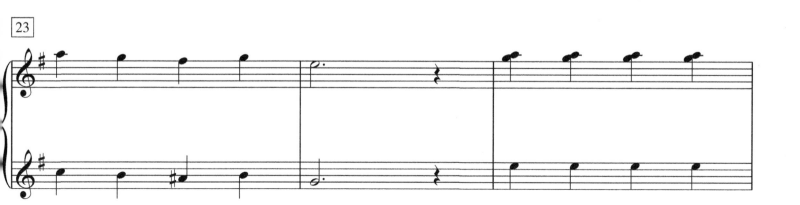

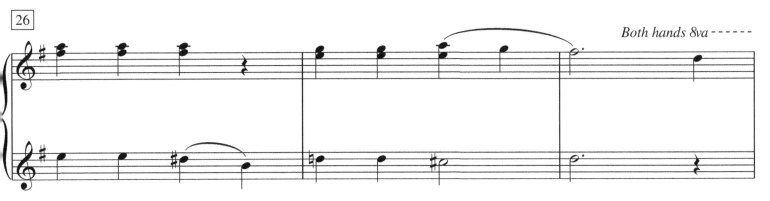

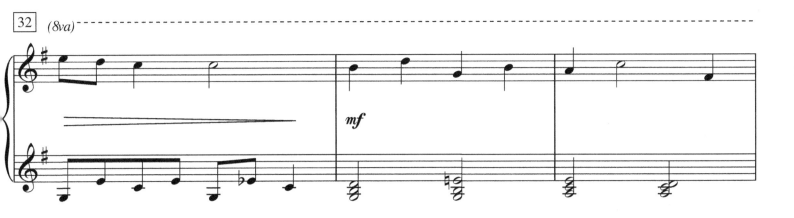

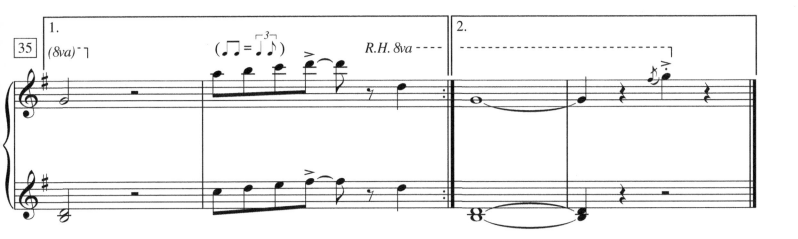

SHAKE ME I RATTLE
(Squeeze Me I Cry)

SECONDO

Words and Music by HAL HACKADY
and CHARLES NAYLOR

Moderately slow

With pedal

SHAKE ME I RATTLE
(Squeeze Me I Cry)

PRIMO

Words and Music by HAL HACKADY
and CHARLES NAYLOR

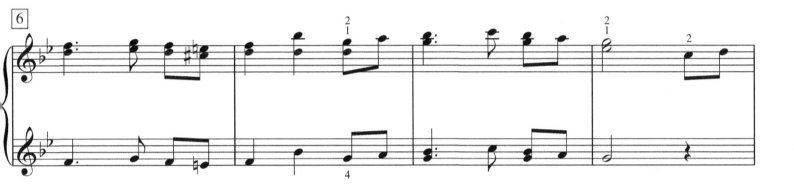

SECONDO

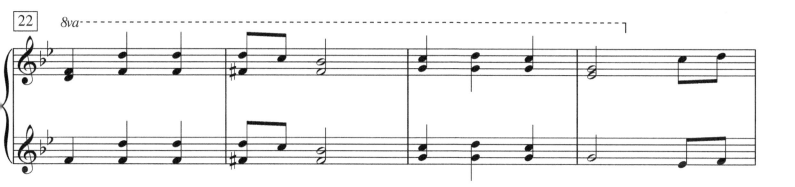

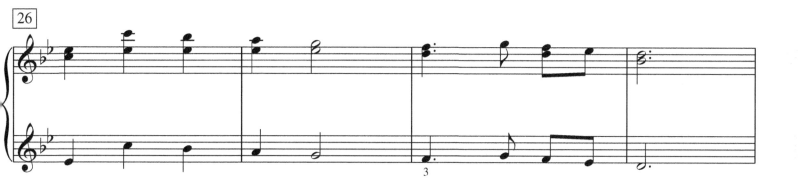

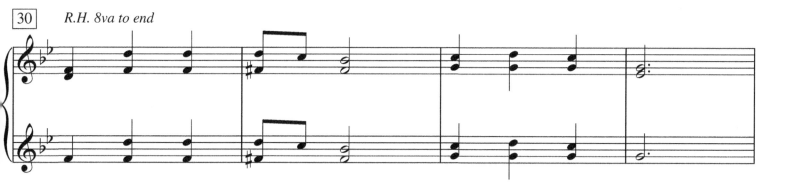

SECONDO

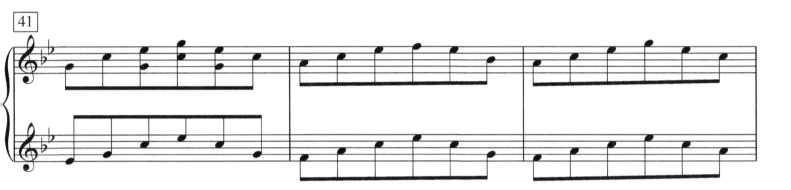

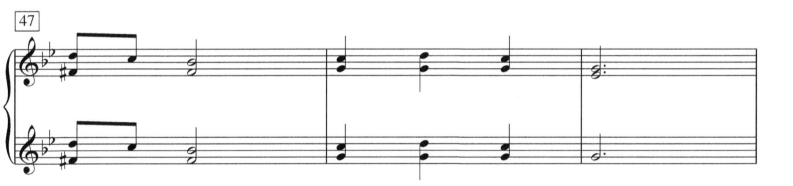

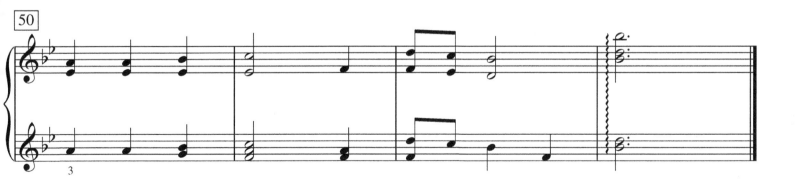

SILVER BELLS
from the Paramount Picture THE LEMON DROP KID

SECONDO

Words and Music by JAY LIVINGSTON
and RAY EVANS

Moderately and smoothly

SILVER BELLS
from the Paramount Picture THE LEMON DROP KID

PRIMO

Words and Music by JAY LIVINGSTON
and RAY EVANS

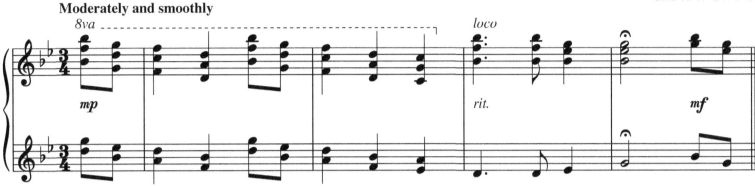

SECONDO

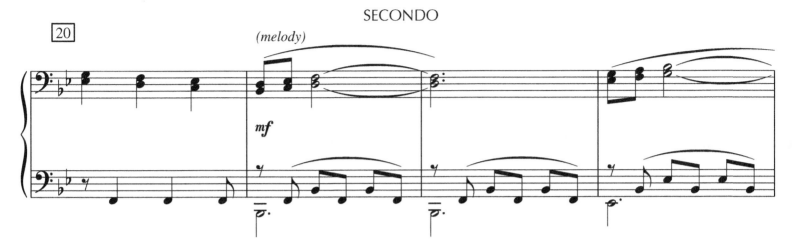

PRIMO

SECONDO

PRIMO

SECONDO

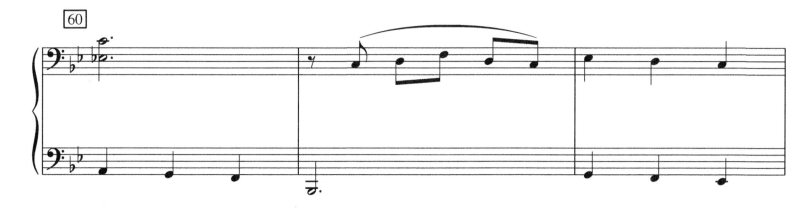

PRIMO

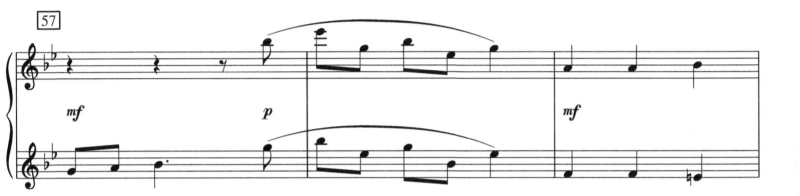

SECONDO

PRIMO

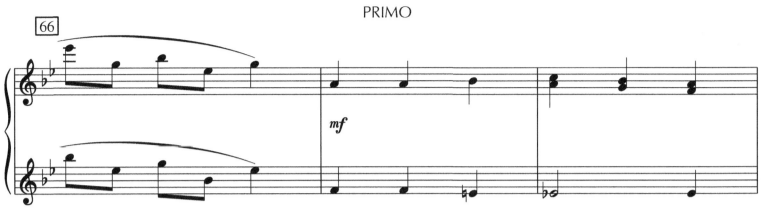

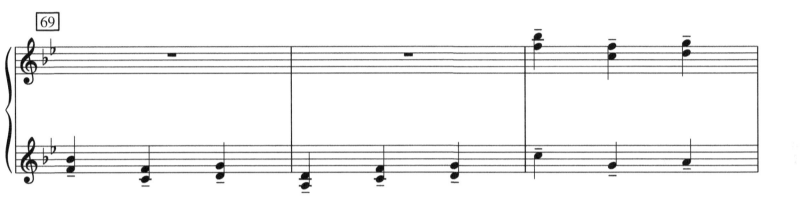

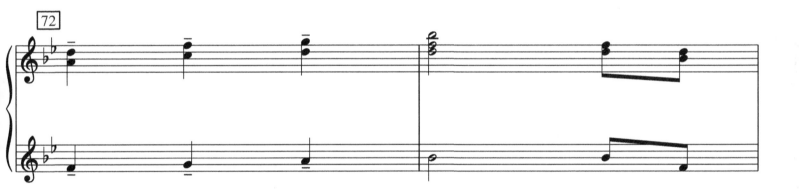

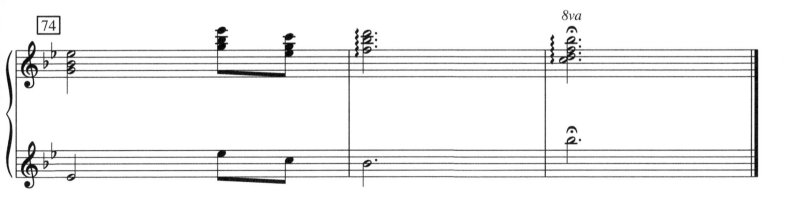

WHAT ARE YOU DOING NEW YEAR'S EVE?

SECONDO

By FRANK LOESSER

WHAT ARE YOU DOING NEW YEAR'S EVE?

PRIMO

By FRANK LOESSER

SECONDO

poco rit.

PRIMO

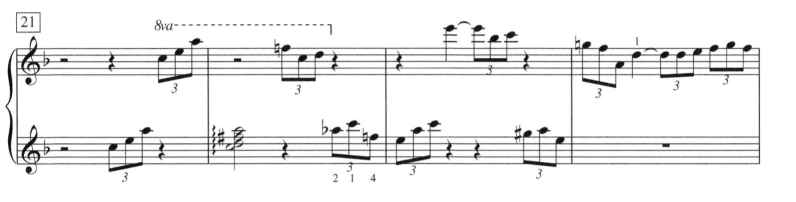

WHITE CHRISTMAS

from the Motion Picture Irving Berlin's HOLIDAY INN

SECONDO

Words and Music by
IRVING BERLIN

Moderately, with warmth

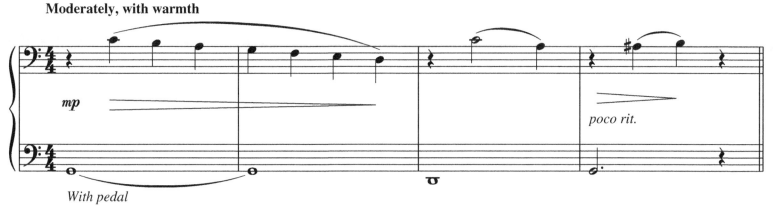

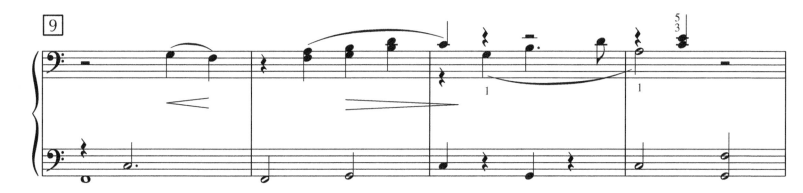

WHITE CHRISTMAS

from the Motion Picture Irving Berlin's HOLIDAY INN

PRIMO

Words and Music by
IRVING BERLIN

Moderately, with warmth

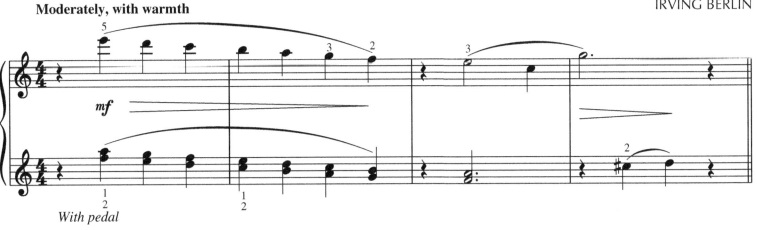

With pedal

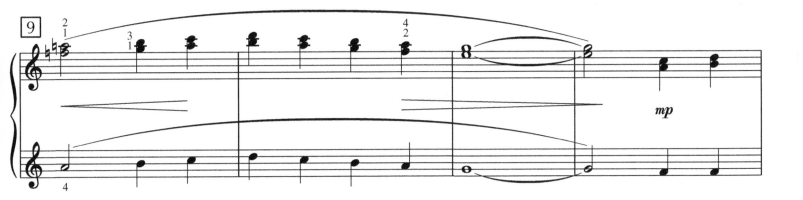

SECONDO

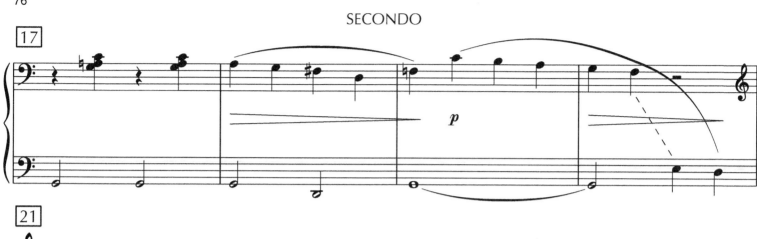

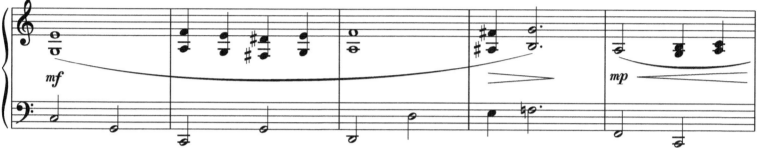

PRIMO

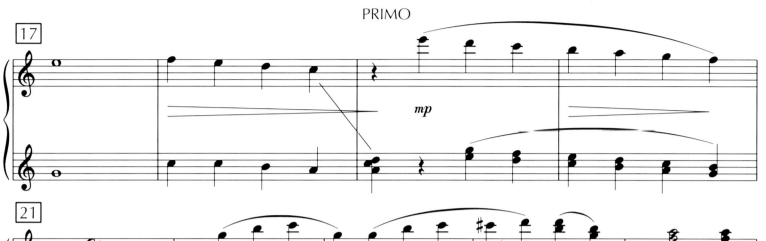

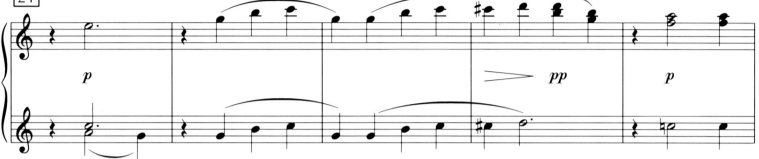

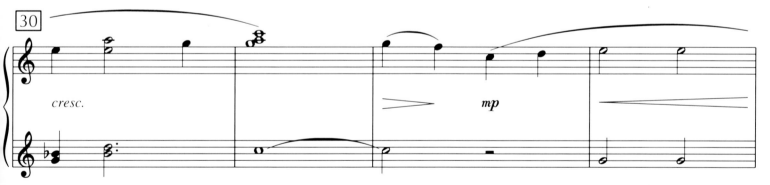

Piano For Two

A VARIETY OF PIANO DUETS FROM HAL LEONARD

THE BEATLES PIANO DUETS – 2ND EDITION

Features 8 arrangements: Can't Buy Me Love • Eleanor Rigby • Hey Jude • Let It Be • Penny Lane • Something • When I'm Sixty-Four • Yesterday.

00290496..................$12.99

GERSHWIN PIANO DUETS

These duet arrangements of 10 Gershwin classics such as "I Got Plenty of Nuttin'," "Summertime," "It Ain't Necessarily So," and "Love Walked In" sound as full and satisfying as the orchestral originals.

00312603..................$12.99

BOB MARLEY FOR PIANO DUET

A unique collection of 10 Marley favorites arranged for piano duet, including: Get Up Stand Up • I Shot the Sheriff • Is This Love • Jamming • No Woman No Cry • One Love • Redemption Song • Stir It Up • and more.

00129926..................$12.99

CONTEMPORARY DISNEY DUETS

8 Disney piano duets to play and perform with a friend! Includes: Almost There • He's a Pirate • I See the Light • Let It Go • Married Life • That's How You Know • Touch the Sky • We Belong Together.

00128259 ....$12.99

THE SOUND OF MUSIC

9 arrangements from the movie/musical, including: Do-Re-Mi • Edelweiss • Maria • My Favorite Things • So Long, Farewell • The Sound of Music • and more.

00290389..................$12.99

RIVER FLOWS IN YOU AND OTHER SONGS ARRANGED FOR PIANO DUET

10 great songs arranged for 1 piano, 4 hands, including the title song and: All of Me (Piano Guys) • Bella's Lullaby • Beyond • Chariots of Fire • Dawn • Forrest Gump - Main Title (Feather Theme) • Primavera • Somewhere in Time • Watermark.

00141055..................$12.99

EASY CLASSICAL DUETS

7 great piano duets to perform at a recital, play-for-fun, or sightread! Titles: By the Beautiful Blue Danube (Strauss) • Eine kleine Nachtmusik (Mozart) • Sleeping Beauty Waltz (Tchaikovsky) • and more.

00145767 Book/Online Audio $10.99

BILLY JOEL FOR PIANO DUET

Includes 8 of the Piano Man's greatest hits. Perfect as recital encores, or just for fun! Titles: Just the Way You Are • The Longest Time • My Life • Piano Man • She's Always a Woman • Uptown Girl • and more.

00141139 ....$14.99

STAR WARS

8 intergalactic arrangements of *Star Wars* themes for late intermediate to early advanced piano duet, including: Across the Stars • Cantina Band • Duel of the Fates • The Imperial March (Darth Vader's Theme) • Princess Leia's Theme • Star Wars (Main Theme) • The Throne Room (And End Title) • Yoda's Theme.

00119405..................$14.99

TAYLOR SWIFT FOR PIANO DUET

Grab your bestie and start playing 8 Taylor Swift favorites arranged for piano duet! Includes: Blank Space • I Knew You Were Trouble • Love Story • Mine • Shake It Off • Today Was a Fairytale • We Are Never Ever Getting Back Together • You Belong with Me.

00142333..................$12.99

Also Available:

HAL LEONARD PIANO DUET PLAY-ALONG SERIES

This great series comes with audio that features separate tracks for the Primo and Secondo parts – perfect for practice and performance! Visit www.halleonard.com for a complete list of titles in the series!

COLDPLAY

Clocks • Paradise • The Scientist • A Sky Full of Stars • Speed of Sound • Trouble • Viva La Vida • Yellow.

00141054..................$14.99

FROZEN

Do You Want to Build a Snowman? • Fixer Upper • For the First Time in Forever • In Summer • Let It Go • Love Is an Open Door • Reindeer(s) Are Better Than People.

00128260..................$14.99

JAZZ STANDARDS

All the Things You Are • Bewitched • Cheek to Cheek • Don't Get Around Much Anymore • Georgia on My Mind • In the Mood • It's Only a Paper Moon • Satin Doll • The Way You Look Tonight.

00290577..................$14.99

FOR MORE INFORMATION, SEE YOUR LOCAL MUSIC DEALER, OR WRITE TO:

HAL•LEONARD® CORPORATION

7777 W. BLUEMOUND RD. P.O. BOX 13819 MILWAUKEE, WI 53213

www.halleonard.com

CELEBRATE THE SEASON
with Christmas Songbooks for Piano from Hal Leonard

17 Super Christmas Hits

This book contains the most popular, most requested Christmas titles: The Christmas Song • Frosty the Snow Man • A Holly Jolly Christmas • Home for the Holidays • I'll Be Home for Christmas • It's Beginning to Look like Christmas • Jingle-Bell Rock • Let It Snow! Let It Snow! Let It Snow! • The Little Drummer Boy • Mister Santa • Sleigh Ride • We Need a Little Christmas • and more.
00240867 Big-Note Piano $9.95
00361053 Easy Piano $9.95

25 Top Christmas Songs

Includes: Blue Christmas • C-H-R-I-S-T-M-A-S • The Christmas Song • The Christmas Waltz • Do You Hear What I Hear • Have Yourself a Merry Little Christmas • Here Comes Santa Claus • Jingle-Bell Rock • Last Christmas • Pretty Paper • Silver Bells • and more.
00490058 Easy Piano $11.95

Best Christmas Music

A giant collection of 62 Christmas favorites: Away in a Manger • Blue Christmas • The Chipmunk Song • The First Noel • Frosty the Snow Man • Grandma Got Run Over by a Reindeer • I Saw Mommy Kissing Santa Claus • Pretty Paper • Silver Bells • Wonderful Christmastime • more.
00310325 Big-Note Piano $14.95

The Best Christmas Songs Ever

A treasured collection of 70 songs: The Christmas Song • Frosty the Snow Man • Grandma Got Run Over by a Reindeer • Here Comes Santa Claus • A Holly Jolly Christmas • I'll Be Home for Christmas • Jingle-Bell Rock • Let It Snow! Let It Snow! Let It Snow! • Santa Claus Is Comin' to Town • more!
00364130 Easy Piano $19.95

Children's Christmas Songs

22 holiday favorites, including: Frosty the Snow Man • Jingle Bells • Jolly Old St. Nicholas • Rudolph, the Red-Nosed Reindeer • Up on the Housetop • and more!
00222547 Easy Piano $7.95

Christmas Pops

THE PHILLIP KEVEREN SERIES
18 holiday favorites: Because It's Christmas • Blue Christmas • Christmas Time Is Here • I'll Be Home for Christmas • Mary, Did You Know? • Rockin' Around the Christmas Tree • Silver Bells • Tennessee Christmas • more.
00311126 Easy Piano $12.95

Christmas Songs

12 songs, including: Caroling, Caroling • Christmas Time Is Here • Do You Hear What I Hear • Here Comes Santa Claus • It's Beginning to Look like Christmas • Little Saint Nick • Merry Christmas, Darling • Mistletoe and Holly • and more.
00311242 Easy Piano Solo.............................$8.95

Christmas Traditions

THE PHILLIP KEVEREN SERIES
20 beloved songs arranged for beginning soloists: Away in a Manger • Coventry Carol • Deck the Hall • God Rest Ye Merry, Gentlemen • Jingle Bells • Silent Night • We Three Kings of Orient Are • more.
00311117 Beginning Piano Solos................$10.99

Greatest Christmas Hits

18 Christmas classics: Blue Christmas • Brazilian Sleigh Bells • The Christmas Song • Do You Hear What I Hear • Here Comes Santa Claus • I Saw Mommy Kissing Santa Claus • Silver Bells • This Christmas • more!
00311136 Big-Note Piano $9.95

Jazz Up Your Christmas

ARRANGED BY LEE EVANS
12 Christmas carols in a fresh perspective. Full arrangements may be played as a concert suite. Songs include: Deck the Hall • The First Noel • God Rest Ye Merry Gentlemen • The Holly and the Ivy • O Christmas Tree • What Child Is This? • and more.
00009040 Piano Solo $9.95

Jingle Jazz

THE PHILLIP KEVEREN SERIES
17 Christmas standards: Caroling, Caroling • The Christmas Song • I'll Be Home for Christmas • Jingle Bells • Merry Christmas, Darling • The Most Wonderful Time of the Year • Rudolph the Red-Nosed Reindeer • We Wish You a Merry Christmas • and more.
00310762 Piano Solo $12.95

100 Christmas Carols

Includes the Christmas classics: Angels We Have Heard on High • Bring a Torch, Jeannette Isabella • Dance of the Sugar Plum Fairy • The First Noel • Here We Come A-Wassailing • It Came upon the Midnight Clear • Joy to the World • Still, Still, Still • The Twelve Days of Christmas • We Three Kings of Orient Are • and more!
00311134 Easy Piano.................................$15.95

The Nutcracker Suite

ARRANGED BY BILL BOYD
7 easy piano arrangements from Tchaikovsky's beloved ballet. Includes "Dance of the Sugar-Plum Fairy."
00110010 Easy Piano..................................$8.95

The Ultimate Series: Christmas

The ultimate collection of Christmas classics includes 100 songs: Carol of the Bells • The Chipmunk Song • Christmas Time Is Here • Do You Hear What I Hear • The First Noel • Gesù Bambino • Happy Xmas (War Is Over) • Jesu, Joy of Man's Desiring • Silver and Gold • What Child Is This? • Wonderful Christmastime • and more.
00241003 Easy Piano.................................$19.95

FOR MORE INFORMATION, SEE YOUR LOCAL MUSIC DEALER, OR WRITE TO:

HAL•LEONARD® CORPORATION
7777 W. BLUEMOUND RD. P.O. BOX 13819 MILWAUKEE, WI 53213
Complete songlists online at **www.halleonard.com**

Prices, contents and availability subject to change without notice.